CAN I REALLY MAKE MONEY ONLINE?

or

10 Totally Legal But Morally Questionable Ways I Earned Cash As A Digital Nomad

By

Amie-Jade Moore

1 - THAT TIME I WAS A PROFESSIONAL GAMBLER 10

2 - THAT TIME I SOLD MY TRASHED SHOES AND PICTURES OF MY FEET TO FETISHISTS 18

3 - THAT TIME I WAS A SPY WORKING IN CASINOS 30

4 - THAT TIME I TRIED SELLING MY DIRTY UNDERWEAR TO STRANGERS..36

5 – THAT TIME I GOT KICKED OUT OF A PYRAMID SCHEME 41

6 - THE TIME I MADE FIFTY SHADES OF GREY LOOK FAMILY FRIENDLY..49

7 - THAT TIME I CONVINCED THE WORLD I WAS AN "INFLUENCER"...55

8 – THAT TIME I TRIED LOSING WEIGHT FOR CASH 62

9 – THAT TIME I SOLD BOOKS FULL OF BLANK PAGES 71

10 – THAT TIME I WROTE A BOOK ABOUT ALL MY ICKY EXPERIENCES...76

Before we go any further, I want to let you know what you're going to find in this book, so you can make an informed decision before you decide to buy it. I'm not going to waste your time, so it's only fair to let you know what you're going to get. I'm a writer and digital content producer from Scotland. This is my story. It's not a self-help book, a coaching book or advice of any kind. I'm also not advertising or advocating. This is what I did. Everything you will read in this book is based on my own experiences and my only intentions are 1) to let people know what could possibly happen if they are inspired by my story and try these money-making schemes too and 2) to make money myself. Because let's be honest. Every book you buy online is there so that someone can make money.

You can also expect honesty from me. I'll cut through the bullshit and I'll tell you the facts. Ok, so I will make them into a story which is readable, but that's to be expected. I am a writer after all. But there are no lies in this book. Everything you read is 100% true. It's also why I thought it might be a good idea to use a pen name because I really don't want a future boss (if I ever have another – I really hope not) to be able to Google me and find all these unusual things I've done in an attempt to make money online. It wouldn't be difficult to find out who I really am, but in the interest of keeping my real life as drama free as possible, just call me Amie-Jade or AJ.

You will find swearing, adult content and situations that you don't want your kids reading. So maybe wait until they're in bed before you pick this up...?

Now, you're probably thinking this is a 15,000-word book, and you've paid $5 for it. That seems like a steep price for what I'm giving you in return, so it had better be good. But what I'm giving you is the chance to hear the truth about some of these money-making schemes so you don't waste your own time and you can invest your energy into what really works. I think that's worth $5, don't you?

*****

My story begins somewhere around 2014. I was a working mother with a career in law and a writing hobby that I'd been pursuing since 2002 that occasionally brought in some cash. I had written a series of cat detective stories that were dripping a little passive income into my bank account.

I decided to leave that job as a paralegal. It wasn't that I was terribly unhappy there, although it wasn't great, if I'm honest. I spent at least half an hour out of every working day crying in the toilets because I worked in probate and wills, which can be emotionally challenging because you're hearing stories about death and dying all the time.

My husband, Fraser, had just suffered a stroke, my toddler son, Bruce, wasn't meeting his milestones and I was finding it increasingly difficult to switch off my brain when leaving the office to do normal stuff like keeping the house clean and tidy. I was at the point where I'd had enough. So, I left, planning to take a few weeks off, go on vacation that spring and then look for a job in summer. Yes, I use the word vacation rather than holiday, even though I am Scottish. It's much nicer to vacate your life than to have a holiday, which makes me think of rainy Mondays in May with shit old movies on TV.

By the autumn of 2015 I hadn't found a job. I had started my own business selling craft perfumes – eau de parfums that I had designed and made myself. That business was bleeding money. We were going through the struggle to get an autism diagnosis for Bruce, I had raging sciatica that was draining me physically and emotionally and preventing me from getting back into work, there were mounting debts, my writing hobby had become a massive source of pressure to get more books out as fast as possible... *breathe* and I was becoming very depressed. Christmas was fast approaching, and I had no way to pay for Santa's visit. So, I did what any other mother would do.

I did whatever I had to.

In that instance, it meant becoming a professional gambler, a decision I have never regretted to this day, but not one that I am particularly proud of. Over the next five years, I tried everything from pyramid schemes to publishing empty books to selling used underwear to fetishists.

If you're raising your eyebrows now and judging me, then you'll understand why I am writing this under a pseudonym. This is not one of those "make money online" books, written by a life coach with a veneer smile, a home in the South Pacific and a passport full of stamps. It's written by a woman who is probably a lot like you. I was a career girl who had a run of strange luck, a lot of unexpected obstacles thrown in her path and who couldn't see a conventional way out. Getting a regular job was not an option. That's why I tried everything that was out there.

In case you want to skip to a particular money-making method, I've included a table of contents below. If you're reading a paperback, there are page numbers and if you're reading the e-book there's a hyperlink to each section.

1 - THAT TIME I WAS A PROFESSIONAL GAMBLER......10

2 - THAT TIME I SOLD MY TRASHED SHOES AND PICTURES OF MY FEET TO FETISHISTS..........................18

3 - THAT TIME I WAS A SPY WORKING IN CASINOS 30

4 - THAT TIME I TRIED SELLING MY DIRTY UNDERWEAR TO STRANGERS 36

5 – THAT TIME I GOT KICKED OUT OF A PYRAMID SCHEME 41

6 - THE TIME I MADE FIFTY SHADES OF GREY LOOK FAMILY FRIENDLY 49

7 - THAT TIME I CONVINCED THE WORLD I WAS AN "INFLUENCER" 55

8 – THAT TIME I TRIED LOSING WEIGHT FOR CASH 62

9 – THAT TIME I SOLD BOOKS FULL OF BLANK PAGES 71

10 – THAT TIME I WROTE A BOOK ABOUT ALL MY ICKY EXPERIENCES 76

Just reading all that back, I know I sound dodgy as fuck, but these are all things that are totally legal, even if they are morally questionable.

You're thinking, that will never happen to me. I'm totally focused and driven. I know exactly where I'm going in life. In reply I'd say, yeah hun, that's nice and I'm happy for you but what happens if:

Your company has mounting debts that you didn't even know about.

Once, an old boss of mine called many employees into a meeting first thing on Monday and they were never seen again. Over the following weeks, people would be called in at 5pm and told to clear their desks because they weren't coming back the next day. After three months we had lost two-thirds of the staff. Been there.

The factory where you work is destroyed in a fire over the weekend and when Monday comes, you don't have a job to go to.
That happened to my grandmother.

There's a global pandemic of Hollywood movie proportions that nobody could have predicted and the café where you work as a waiter simply can't open for health reasons.
How many of you reading this can relate to that? My brother-in-law can.

You have a bad back and one day, you wake up and you can hardly move.
You don't remember doing anything strenuous... although there was that one weird sneeze that kind of twinged the day before. You're out of action and in physio for MONTHS. Possibly years. And then the people who are supposed to help you let you down

in a big way... yeah, you'll have to skip to chapter eight for more on that.

You've spent a decade building a career for yourself and it's going great. Then your spouse or child has an accident that again, nobody could have predicted.
Maybe someone becomes dependent on you after a stroke or heart attack. You must make a heart-wrenching decision - the career you worked so hard to achieve or taking care of your family member and kissing goodbye to your regular, reliable-ish income.

Whatever your issue is, I've been there. I know how it feels, and I know how powerless you become in these situations. So, grab a coffee, get cosy in a comfy chair and buckle up because some of these stories will... hmm, I was going to say make your hair stand on end, but we've all been through 2020. We're probably at the stage where nothing can shock us. So, hopefully these will just make you laugh!

1 - THAT TIME I WAS A PROFESSIONAL GAMBLER

Also known as the first time I had a terrible idea, and nobody was around to talk me out of it

This is the time I can pinpoint as when my troubles *really* began. It was September 2015 and my fragrance business had just launched. I had spent the previous year taking an unbelievable number of perfumery courses, designing fragrances, having meetings with events managers at local hotels and locking down a partnership with a perfume house in London. I was going to host perfume making parties, which would take me halfway to my dream of designing bespoke perfumes for the women of the west of Scotland. Who wants to smell like a celebrity when you can smell like the most glamorous version of yourself? Why wouldn't you want to have your own signature scent?

The problem is nobody does. Everyone wants to smell like the bottle that someone from reality TV has endorsed, just like a hundred thousand other women who bought that same bottle from Superdrug. The business model was a failure, the partnership wasn't the glitterfest I imagined it to be and after my son's autism diagnosis earlier that month, my entire family had turned on me. In their minds, if the diagnosis hadn't happened, we could all have told ourselves that he was fine and ignored the milestone delays for a little while longer. I'd known in my heart for a while that we were looking at autism and that to give him the best chance to have a happy, independent life, I would need to take the first step and get him diagnosed to secure the right therapies, but they weren't emotionally prepared for such a huge shift in what they pictured his future to be, and I was the target for their anger.

So, I found myself very alone and in a bigger financial mess than I had ever been in at any point in my life. I didn't have anyone to talk to about it, except for my husband. And Fraser, like me, didn't have a clue what we were going to do about this. We were the ones everyone else came to for a loan. We were the solid, dependable couple. How could it have happened to us? And how did I get to a point where I couldn't confide in my family, or ask my parents for help? It's definitely not the worst thing that has ever happened to me but being in such a scary place financially is up there in the top five worst things.

We were due to go on holiday in October of that year, and I had no way to pay for the petrol to get us there. I needed £50 fast. I remember the Rugby World Cup was happening around then, and there were plenty of ads on TV about free bets to celebrate the tournament starting. I was intrigued. If it was a free bet, did that mean I could potentially win without risk?

I'm not a huge gambler, although I do enjoy it occasionally. I don't drink, smoke or do drugs, so I've always told myself it's absolutely fine to indulge now and again on major sporting events like the Grand National or the World Cup. As a younger woman, I'd visit casinos if I was on vacation, and have occasional trips to the arcade, but that was the limit of my gambling knowledge. I didn't want to visit an actual bookmaker at that time because I was feeling quite depressed and couldn't handle seeing anyone I knew. So, I Googled online bookmakers, hoping to find a blog or review site that would tell me the best one to sign up to and maybe I'd get a free bet offer. That's when I accidentally stumbled upon a site with a lengthy article about something called "matched betting." And that was when things started to look rosy.

Matched betting is a legal, but frowned upon, way of making a guaranteed profit from gambling websites - so long as you stick to the system and don't actually take any gambles. It works by placing two simultaneous bets twice and extracting the profit from free bet offers quite frequently dished out by bookmakers.

For example, say there is a bookmaker called Smiths. Smiths are offering a free £20 bet to anyone who bets at least £30 on that day's Man Utd. match. So, you place your £30 bet on Man Utd to win. Then you go to a betting exchange (there are plenty of them online) and you bet that Man Utd. will not win. So, if Man Utd. win, you win at Smiths, the bookmaker. If they draw or lose, you win at the betting exchange. No matter what happens, you've probably only lost a small, acceptable amount.

Then, you take the free bet, and you do the same. You bet on a rugby match, for example, Scotland v. Wales. You use your freebie to bet that Scotland will win. Then you use the betting exchange to bet that Scotland will not win. So, if they draw or lose, you win at the betting exchange and if they win, you win at Smiths. You have then made a profit.

There are calculators online that allow you to enter the odds and the amounts you're betting, and they'll tell you the best amounts to place on each market to create maximum profit.

It wasn't really gambling, but because the money was coming from a bookmaker, that made it gambling in the eyes of the law - which made it tax free. Plus, the money was coming into my account in a matter of hours or days. It was quick, it was certain (so long as I stuck to the system) and there were dozens of free bet offers out there. I even found a blog written by a man who updated every day with all the free bet offers he was finding all over the world.

For the next three months, I signed up to more and more bookmakers daily, creating accounts, claiming free bets and raking in the cash. I made enough to keep us going and pay for Christmas that year. I became quite knowledgeable about South American and African football leagues and obscure sporting events like the World Handball Championships. My family (who, by that time were starting to get their heads around the diagnosis and were behaving the way a family should again), were completely baffled as to how and why I had become so keen on international football leagues. I recall a conversation with my octogenarian grandfather on New Year's Day about which bookie had the best odds for a horse race and I raised a few eyebrows. Nobody questioned me though.

Obviously, by that point, I had accepted that my perfume business wasn't going to work. I kept the partnership going with the perfume house in London until the end of 2016 but as soon as I started matched betting, I stopped ploughing money into the business. My little perfumery seemed like more of a gamble than anything I did on gambling websites.

All good things must come to an end though and this certainly did. There were three reasons for that.

I ran out of free bet offers. At first, they were plentiful and from British sites that I trusted. As soon as I started looking further afield, the terms and conditions became baffling. I remember one Eastern European site that allowed you to claim a free bet, but you had to then bet eight times that amount in order to withdraw the money you had won, which made it a waste of time and depleted the winnings.

The bookies aren't daft. They know who's only visiting the site to claim the free bet offers and if you're doing that, it's almost certain that you're matched betting. One bookie banned me from claiming free bet offers. It's now 2020, and they still haven't allowed me one single free bet. Fraser signed up to the site too, thinking he would give it a go, but because he lives at the same address, this made him ineligible for the offers. One per household. And they check! There is also the chance that the betting exchange is owned by the same organisation as the site you're claiming free bets from - I made that mistake a couple of times too.

The third reason was that it was exhausting and demoralising. I found myself investing more and more time into looking for these offers, calculating, checking results... it wasn't a passive income. This was a full-time job, but it didn't pay as much as a full-time job. One afternoon, when I was dropping Bruce off at nursery, I realised that I hadn't placed one particular bet at an exchange and had to do it on my phone, standing outside the nursery or I would lose £50. If I waited until after the game started, the odds might change, and I wouldn't be able to claw it back. Bruce was late for nursery - only by two or three minutes. But when I went inside and apologised for being late, I realised that I couldn't tell the teachers why. It's not the kind of thing you can publicly admit. I felt like the worst mother in the world. I had started matched betting because I needed to find a way to buy Christmas presents for him. I'd always said that I was doing it **for him** but if it was making me late for his nursery drop off, how was that benefitting him? That was the moment when I knew I had to find another way.

I discussed it with my husband, and we agreed that the professional gambling career would be put on hold indefinitely. I'd had a good run. It was time to move on to a different career.

PROFIT MADE: £846

ICK FACTOR: 4/10

CHANCES OF DOING IT AGAIN: 4/10

Overall, this was a profitable scheme and I have already said that I don't regret doing it. Without matched betting, there would have been no Christmas in 2015. But it didn't feel like safe income and I definitely wasn't able to tell anyone about what I had been doing. I logged out of those gambling sites for good in January 2016 and got to work on my cat mysteries again.

2 - THAT TIME I SOLD MY TRASHED SHOES AND PICTURES OF MY FEET TO FETISHISTS

Also known as the reason why the woman in the post office hates me

Some of you are seeing the title of this chapter and you've got "*the ick.*" You're ready to close it down and give me a one-star review. At best, you're laughing your head off and desperate to hear what I'm going to say. Either way, now you'll understand why I've used a pseudonym.

Time moved on and we're now in 2016. I occasionally got to host a perfume party, which never earned me more than £80 a time. My only source of income was writing. Freelance work was thin on the ground and I was becoming an unreliable worker. I was constantly tired as my little one still wasn't sleeping through the night, despite being five years old at that point. I was taking on jobs and forgetting about them, falling out with people I was working for because I was grumpy and inflexible, and I was in constant pain from sciatica. Life wasn't much fun in 2016 but somehow, I was managing to hold it together just enough so that nobody could see the cracks. And unbelievably, family members were still asking us for loans, because those cracks were so well hidden.

We got a phone call one night from my stepson, Jasper. He had an eBay shop that brought in over a grand a month, as well as a full-time job and his wife's benefits (she is registered blind and gets disability benefits) but for some reason, he urgently needed to borrow money. Despite being overdrawn ourselves, my husband agreed to loan Jasper £100. When we visited his home to give him the money, we saw his eBay store's "stock" in the spare room. He was selling all sorts of things, from used computer games, to old coins, to slippers that his wife, Jenna, had grown tired of.

'Does anyone buy slippers?' I asked.

'Of course. People will buy anything,' Jasper said.

'But what do they do with slippers? These have got a hole in them.'

'Not for me to ask,' Jasper shrugged. 'Although they don't sell unless they smell.'

'What?' Fraser and I said in unison.

Jasper went on to relate a story about the last time he sold a pair of shoes on eBay. He received a message from an interested buyer who wanted to know what they smelled like. Thinking that they would have to be wearable, Jasper told him that the shoes were in great condition. The potential buyer lost interest. He only wanted them if they reeked of foot. We laughed, but the wheels were turning in my mind. Could that be the next money-making scheme?

I had a whole bundle of shoes lying at home from the days when I used to buy a new pair every week - those days of having plenty of disposable income were long gone. The problem was, most of them had sky-scraper heels and since my back was in terrible condition, the shoes wouldn't be worn again any time soon.

I shrugged off the idea, thinking that it was pointless to even consider it. I was still in the frame of mind that told me a job was how you made money. Or a business. You couldn't make it by any other means. I archived the idea away in the same place in my mind where I put smear tests and failed perfumeries. I carried on writing cat detective shorts.

Until around Christmas.

It was after midnight. I had posted a picture of a new pair of slippers I got from Fraser online and suddenly a stranger slid into my Twitter DMs. His name was Steve and he wanted to know what I was doing with my old ones. He asked if he could buy them. I decided it was too much of a coincidence, after the conversation with Jasper. The universe was trying to tell me something, so I replied to him.

'I still have them. How much would you pay?'

'I'd make it worth your while. I'll pay a lot,' was all Steve said in response.

I switched off my phone and went to bed. When I woke the next morning, it was the first thing on my mind. I was still broke. I was in so much pain I could barely walk some days and Bruce still needed a lot of care and attention (and was only sleeping until 4am each morning), meaning I couldn't hold down a job. I wasn't even managing to freelance successfully. There was no fairy godmother coming to change my life. Things were getting more and more complicated, and Steve was offering me a temporary fix.

I sent Steve a picture of my old slippers and then put them in a plastic bag while I waited for him to reply, telling me if he was still interested.

There were a lot of unanswered questions about this kind of transaction. Could I make a lot of money? Did I have to put my home address on the parcel I sent out to the buyer? Do you have to declare a private transaction as income? If Steve was involved in a violent crime in his home and they found my shoes and my DNA at the crime scene, would I be implicated?

Ok, maybe it's just me who thinks along those lines. That's my writer's brain kicking into gear. I still think it's a valid question though.

The most important question was **how would I feel about myself** if I did this? Would I feel dirty? Is it a type of prostitution? Am I a sex-worker now??? I consider myself to be quite open-minded and I don't judge other people's sexual preferences, but I have my limits. I thought this could be one of them.

When I brought up the subject with a friend, Linda, she was quick to shut it down. She told me that it was perverse and that social services would take Bruce away from me. I was a little upset and so I talked it over with Fraser. He pointed out that selling shoes to someone online is no different to selling a dress on eBay. How did I know, at any point, that selling a dress to someone meant they would be wearing it and not masturbating over it? Nobody knows what happens once you sell something on eBay, so you must treat it like the cold business transaction it is and don't ask questions.

It wasn't like I need to ask many questions anyway. Steve, my potential buyer, was clearly a foot fetishist. I could see on the public information I could view on Twitter, that Steve was interacting with a dominatrix. On her own page, she had been posting screenshots of him sending money into her Circle account. She called these payments, "tributes." In return, all he wanted was to be told how pathetic he was and to get occasional glimpses of her feet. She would tag him in the photos for all her 20,000+ followers to see to add to his humiliation.

I did get a response from Steve and he agreed to pay £50 for the old slippers. I told him to send me the money via PayPal and send his address and I would post them out to him in a zip-lock bag to retain any scent, even though they didn't actually smell too bad. Unfortunately, the transaction didn't go ahead. He vanished from Twitter. So did the dominatrix. I take it somebody reported them. Probably Linda. So, I logged onto my eBay account and listed the slippers instead.

I listed slippers, boots and stilettos, and just for a laugh, a pair of laddered tights with several snags in the legs. I wanted to see what I could get away with. Within a few minutes, my views for each item were into double figures. Within an hour, my inbox was full of messages to answer. I had quite a few watchers.

Things you should know before I go on:

1. eBay and other family friendly auction sites are not happy about people doing this and they aim to discourage it

2. When listing the shoes, I described size, colour, type etc. I stuck to facts and didn't get too saucy. Trust me, the potential buyers knew exactly what I was up to without any blatant or explicit descriptions

3. I made sure I described them as "will be cleaned to meet eBay regulations before sending" and didn't use phrases like "well-worn" because this is a red flag to eBay

4. Although I listed tights once and got away with it, all subsequent times I posted them earned me a blocked listing

My one big mistake the first time I listed a pair of shoes was saying, "Any questions, feel free to message me." This opened the door for dialogue and when they had asked everything they possibly could about the shoes, they attempted to talk dirty to me - I ignored them at that point.

I always made sure I showed my husband every single message because the more I received, the more worried I got about one of the buyers getting my address and one (or any) of them being a threat to my safety. It wasn't too much of a stretch of the imagination. It could easily have happened.

I didn't want to take any of the conversations off eBay and onto email, but one man did give me his email address and the conversation went like this:

Him: Will they be cleaned before you send them?

Me: Do you want them to be cleaned?

Him: I'd love to be told to do that myself

I showed Fraser the message exchange and asked him for guidance on how to respond. He said I was on my own. I told the guy to make sure he was the highest bidder. I didn't hear from him again. He probably went and had a wank over the stern tone of my message.

I was inundated with requests for pictures of my feet too. I by-passed Linda this time and went into a group chat with my old school friends, Chloe and Lianna, who are probably the most open-minded friends I have. Lianna runs an erotic blog and Chloe photographs nude models.

Lianna: Do it. Stop overthinking it. This is easy cash.

Chloe: Just fucking do it.

Amie-Jade: Really? You think it would be alright?

Lianna: It's only feet. It's not like you're flashing your snatch. Nobody's going to identify you from your feet.

Amie-Jade: True. Would you do it?

Chloe: Yeah, because it's easy money and I'm not fucking stupid.

The truth is the pictures *were* easy money. He wanted one hundred snaps for £40, showing the feet from a variety of different angles. Fraser and I made a lot of jokes about how we could photograph his feet instead (which are quite hairy, and I like to call them "hobbit feet") and send those. I was tempted to do that for a laugh, but I didn't want to ruin the chance of repeat business. Can you guess what happened though?

I showed him the first picture as a sample, to get the money into my account before I sent him the rest. He declined. Apparently, he wanted my feet, but he wanted a little more than that too, something he had failed to mention when we made our agreement. I chalked it down to experience, cursed Chloe for encouraging me to do it in the first place and logged back into eBay.

I had posted numerous pairs of shoes and they were all gaining watchers. Some were gaining bids. Since I had started ignoring everyone who was trying to talk dirty, I had only one question in my inbox on the day that all my auctions were due to end.

Buyer: Do you do anything with them before selling?

Me: They'll be cleaned to meet eBay's regulations before selling as stated in the description.

Buyer: Do you do anything else with them?

Me: I'll place them in a zip-lock bag to prevent damage in transit.

Buyer: Anything else?

Me: Well, what do you fucking want me to do with them?

Buyer: I want you to make them wet.

I sat there, re-reading the message a few times, thinking that if I washed them, they would get wet, but that would mean they would be heavier, and I'd have to bump up the postage. Then I realised that he meant he wanted them smeared in vaginal fluids.

So, this is basically what happens when you try to sell shoes online. You must be prepared for that and if you're willing to dedicate time to filtering out those conversations, it can be profitable. However,

I'm not. I was too sore, too tired and too sad to keep this going. And after some of the message exchanges, I honestly had never felt so dry downstairs in my life.

You also must prepare yourself for the possibility that you may only make a small amount on some pairs. My first auction closed at less than £10. It was for a pair of black lace up Dr. Marten heels I used to wear to my office job which were sold to a very formal and appropriate man in Ipswich who described them in his positive feedback as a "lovely purchase." Every time I see the words "lovely purchase" in any review online now, I think of my buyer in Ipswich and wonder if he still has them.

PROFIT MADE: £150

ICK FACTOR: 8/10

CHANCES OF DOING IT AGAIN: 1/10 (I did make a little money, after all)

This scheme became public because I wrote about it on my blog. It's my most viewed post. Most of those views come from women researching how to make money by selling their shoes online. I eventually had to disable comments since the girls in question started leaving their contact details for men to get in touch to buy shoes. Unfortunately, some people from the small village where I live have read the blog and the woman from the post office snarls at me every time she sees me in the street, especially if I'm sending a shoe-box sized parcel. If she only knew some of the other shit I've done...

The income noted above is for a month's work. I have no doubts if I had continued with this it would have continued to be lucrative, especially if I had trawled second-hand shops to get old shoes they couldn't or wouldn't re-sell since they were trashed.

3 - THAT TIME I WAS A SPY WORKING IN CASINOS

Also known as the time there was so much paperwork that I can't take James Bond seriously now because I know what his job really involves

Ok, so saying I was a "spy" is kind of hyperbolic. It's not like I worked for MI6 or anything, although an agency paid me to enter a building, act out a scenario and report back with my findings. So, yes. Technically I was a spy.

I was a little further along 2016 by this point and still looking for ways to make money that didn't involve a job, either full-time or part-time. My sciatica was seriously wearing me down and the summer passed in a blur of painkillers and moving from chair to chair around the house trying to find a comfortable position to write in. Nothing worked so I occupied myself by running errands for my elderly neighbour, Maggie, because as soon as I sat down, I would cry from the pain.

Maggie was 93 and had lived a fantastic life. At that point, I'm happy to say she was my best friend. I would sometimes go to the supermarket for her and pick up some essentials - her idea of essentials included banana milk, pizza and spring rolls. I honestly don't know how she got to live to that age because she ate and drank everything she wasn't supposed to.

She would always ask how my health was and I would reply with the standard, 'Fine, except for my back and my left leg. They're always sore.' She was the only person who took my pain seriously, and the only person who understood the financial predicament. She would come up with weird ideas though.

'Why don't you sell cards?'

'Cards?' I'd reply.

'Aye. Cards. You're very creative. You could make cards.'

And then a week later this birthday card making kit would appear in her living room, which she just happened to have lying around, and wanted me to have. The same happened with various other crafts, like candle making and jewellery making, and they would be gifted with the standard encouragement; I was very creative, so I should make something and sell it.

Yes, I'm a creative *writer*. I'm not an artist. But I politely thanked her for the kits she would give me every couple of weeks, gave the crafts a go and passed on my efforts to her, so she could see how terrible I was at literally everything.

What I didn't tell Maggie was that I had stumbled upon another idea and it wasn't exactly a new one. I'd been mystery shopping since 2007. Most of the jobs I undertook didn't pay. They would reimburse expenses but the only incentive to accept the job was a free meal, or a free visit somewhere.

Then some jobs appeared on the agency website that were intriguing. They wanted someone who wasn't a member of a casino, but wouldn't mind becoming a member, to sign up, have a meal in the casino and then act out some scenarios. They would provide £50 to gamble with, and all winnings could be kept.

Jackpot! I could keep anything I earned. The sky was the limit. In the meantime, I would keep crafting anything that Maggie gave me and hope that I found a hidden talent.

So, one night in the summer of 2016, Fraser and I got our glad rags on and went to the casino. We were going through a sticky patch and needed time together and we were glad to let my parents take Bruce for the evening. To be fair, I think Bruce was glad to get some time away from us too. The money situation coupled with my back problems were a strain on our relationship and we knew things had to improve soon or we would end up in real trouble. Sadly, I don't think that's uncommon in marriages where there are debts or money problems.

It was easy to sign up as a member of the casino. There were some forms to fill in and I had to provide identification, then we were taken upstairs and shown to the restaurant area. I always felt a bit nervous when I was mystery shopping, but this time I felt more so. I think that was because there was so much cash at stake.

After the meal, I started acting out the scenarios they had given me, some of which were truly ridiculous. I had to approach a member of staff and ask him to show me how to work some of the gaming machines, including a one-armed bandit.

'So, how does this one work?' I asked.

The guy looked at me like I was an imbecile.

'This one,' I said again, pointing to it.

'You put a coin in here,' he said putting a finger to the slot, 'Then you pull this. If you win, it will spit money out. If you don't win, it won't.'

'Right. So, it's that easy?' I said, my face flushing furiously.

He sighed and looked at me, knowing that I was either unbelievably stupid, or a mystery shopper. I turned away from him and walked toward the roulette table.

Four times that summer I had to sign up and become a member of different casinos, and each time, acting dumb became more and more excruciating. I became quite proficient at roulette - not that it's hard, as well as some of the other games. I practised on the online casinos, on sites where I still had money that had to be rolled over several times before I could withdraw it – a throwback from my shady matched betting days.

The biggest problem was that I had to spend the money before I could claim it back, and I didn't have a lot to spare. So, although I was able to claim £50 back for gambling expenses, I had to have £50 to begin with and once I spent only £32 because it was all I had. Anything I won didn't feel like a profit because I had spent it to begin with and on one occasion, I lost the receipt for my chips, so I couldn't claim.

Being a spy, working the casinos of Scotland sounded a lot more glamorous than it was and it only lasted a short time because each mystery shopper who went there had to be a new member. It was basically an investigation into how they treated newbies and how easy it was to sign up compared to other casinos in the area. They also wanted to know how people who had no knowledge of gambling were going to be treated by the staff, except I was an ex-professional gambler and it showed. When the work dried up, I was more than a little relieved to be going back to photographing bananas in the supermarket for my mystery shopping tasks.

PROFIT MADE: £40

ICK FACTOR: 2/10

CHANCES OF DOING IT AGAIN: 0/10

There haven't been any opportunities to go back to the casinos on the mystery shopping board and I'm happy to continue photographing bananas. Although I'm a member of every casino in the area, I've never gone back.

4 - THAT TIME I TRIED SELLING MY DIRTY UNDERWEAR TO STRANGERS

Also known as the time I went too far trying to make money and ended up damaging my mental health

Buckle up, it's not going to be a nice chapter. There are times when things get so desperate and so frustrating that you start to lose perspective. This is one of those times. I'm going to set the scene for you...

It's May or June 2017. I can't remember exactly. I've offered to work on a friend's blog for him and keep it running while he is adjusting to new fatherhood. Except, when I said £5 per blog post, I thought I would be simply uploading, which would take 15-20 minutes a post. It turns out I was spending an hour and a half on each post, which is a depressing situation to be in, writing about things you're not interested in for shit money.

I'm also at my lowest point pain-wise. I can't stand. I can't sit. I can't lie down. I'm in constant pain. My GP has not once given me a prescription for painkillers and the referral for physiotherapy still hasn't resulted in even one appointment. It's been two and a half years since I first visited my GP. I phone the clinic in tears and beg them for pain relief. The private osteopath I was seeing is sick of me and doesn't get why I'm not getting better. I doubt he cares either. He just wants rid of me because I'm making him look incompetent (that is not fact, it's opinion based on the parting words and look he gave me – this man hates me. To be fair, I'm not that keen on him either).

I'm spending my free time writing blogs about how suicidal I am and how the thought of one day getting to Azerbaijan is giving me a goal to look forward to. Like... Azerbaijan? I'm out of it. I'm off my head and delirious with pain.

My last cat story sold depressingly poorly and after calculating the hours I worked and how much money I made in royalties, I've worked out that I made six US cents per hour.

Then I hear that I'm not being paid the benefits I applied for. They give me a small interim payment and say they want to monitor my freelance income for a little while longer. They give me forms to fill in... forms that confuse me. I have a university education and I can't understand these forms. I spend my days crying.

I look for other ways to make money again and I stumble upon another truly terrible idea. Orange Is the New Black is the latest big thing on Netflix and apparently the prisoners sell their panties. Well, I could do that, couldn't I? I wear panties.

I don't know if I can even bring myself to write this. I've spent a few hundred words waffling on about what a dark place I was in, because I simply don't want to remember what happened, but I feel like I need to. This is a memoir, albeit a strange one that will probably be bought by hustlers and people looking to get rich quick, and I must document this part of my journey because it was the trough. It was the rags part of my rags to riches story.

There's a site that I can't mention, because I don't think this book would get past Amazon's review process if I did name it. It would probably be advertising or endorsing. I mean, I can mention eBay because that's family friendly, but not this site. Anyway, there's a site that is a marketplace for used panty sellers and buyers and without giving it much thought at all, because by this point, I was desperate and would do anything, I made a fake email account, under a fake name and set up a fake account on this site. The name I used? Amie-Jade Moore. That's where the name I used for this book comes from. It was a random name I made up on the spot for selling dirty knickers.

The idea behind this site is that you sign up, post pictures of your used knickers, sometimes worn and sometimes not, create a profile where you basically tell the world you're a hot 21-year-old virgin who likes to work out, even if you're 50 and only run if someone's chasing you. People will buy your panties and you will make money. You don't disclose your name or address, and everything is very hush-hush and discrete.

I've always denied signing up to this. But I did it. I read a story online about a woman who was paid £3,000 for one pair of panties. It was too tempting an opportunity to walk away from. Fraser knew all about it. He said that if it worked, he would sign up and sell his too. There were plenty of men on the site selling their underwear as well. And it looked like they were making money.

I admit, I didn't give this as much thought as I gave anything else. The idea came to me at a point when I would have done literally anything for the chance of making £3,000. Even £50 would have been delightful. After a week though, I removed the listing, closed my account on the marketplace site and never went back.

PROFIT MADE: £0

ICK FACTOR: 10/10

CHANCES OF DOING IT AGAIN: 0/10

Perhaps the only thing more depressing than the fact that I really did sign up and try to sell my panties online, was the fact that nobody viewed my page. Not one person liked the look of Amie-Jade

Moore's knickers. I wrote a few more blogs about Azerbaijan and took up chaos magick. They seemed like healthier ways of expressing how hopeless I felt than humiliating myself by trying to sell my dirty knickers to randoms.

I still practise chaos magick, by the way. And I still haven't been to Azerbaijan.

5 – THAT TIME I GOT KICKED OUT OF A PYRAMID SCHEME

Also known as the point when I realised that I had to stop telling people I was a writer

It's now summer 2017 and the money situation is worse than it's ever been. Fraser and I submit PPI claims and win them, and they pay for a nice little cheap holiday in October that year and for some private physiotherapy. I have, at this point, decided to turn my back on doctors and osteopaths and the physiotherapy clinic I begin visiting is welcoming and – gotta be honest here, it was the turning point.

My new physio is called Andrea and she brightens my otherwise dark days. I tell her about everything that's been happening, without frills or window dressing and I even confide in her about the time someone tried to attack me in a public toilet eight years before that. She clearly thinks I am mental, but she likes that and seems to genuinely want to help me. She encourages me to keep writing my cat stories, so I do.

In the waiting room of this new clinic, I overhear people talking about a pyramid scheme. It's something I've encountered before. An old friend, Sally, was selling health supplements a few years back. She was mad keen on the company she was working for and introduced me to some of her "colleagues" and uplines. I went to a couple of conferences with her and considered signing up myself. This was before I started my perfumery, which by this point, is a long-forgotten memory.

I went home from the physio clinic and looked up this cosmetics company/pyramid scheme online. It's a household name and is trusted and respected. I've even used their products myself. It's not Avon, by the way. It's another brand, with lots of high-street shops in the UK.

The thing that attracted me to the pyramid scheme wasn't the money this time, although it seemed like a great way to bring in some income. It was the companionship and the support. That was something that had been sorely lacking in my life. I didn't have great friends.

- ❖ I had Linda, who would poo-poo every idea I had, frighten me half to death with worst-case scenario consequences, yet never come up with a better idea
- ❖ I had Chloe and Lianna, who were encouraging me to do all the most depraved things in the name of making a few quid
- ❖ I had Stuart, who was still paying me £5 for every blog post I wrote – some of them took two hours

- I had Sally, who had left her first pyramid scheme, and her second and signed up to her third by this point and got more and more enthusiastic with every new business she got involved with
- I had Maggie, who was now starting to give me random fruit from her kitchen instead of crafting supplies, telling me her granddaughter who worked in Starbucks was a lawyer (barista/barrister, potato/po-tah-toh... same thing) and still claimed to be 93
- I had Candice. She's a bit of a wild card and in much the same position I was in. Except she took her money-making activities into real life. One day I was at her house catching up over a tea and a chat and a random guy turned up. She seemed to know him. She asked me to watch her kids for ten minutes and she went upstairs with him. When she came back down, her cheeks were flushed, and she stuffed a few notes into her wallet. I asked no questions. I really didn't have to. It was obvious what was going on.
- And now I had Andrea, who wasn't really a mate, but was a stabilising influence in my life.

I remembered Sally being really fired up about the friendships she had made through her company. She said they would be friends for life. They were all extremely positive and supportive of each other. Positivity is very seductive. There was no criticism, no shaming and just pure joy when you looked at their social media profiles. These people were liquid sunshine. They all had a tragic back-story that was solved by joining the scheme and I wanted some of that in my life. I wanted to be part of their world. (You're singing the song form the Little Mermaid now, aren't you?)

I signed up. I bought the starter kit on my credit card. The kit came through in the mail and I was added to a Facebook group with the rest of my "team." Within minutes, I had dozens of friend requests on Facebook from the other girls and I had been added to a secret group. For a lonely woman with massive problems and few friends she could draw support from this was ***thrilling***. I had found my tribe.

For a day or so, it all went well. Because this company was a household name, when I announced I was now selling their products, I ended up getting a bit of interest from friends and family. They wanted to have a look at the catalogue, some promised to put in orders. About half a dozen did in that first week.

Then the wheels came off. Of course, they did. It wouldn't be that easy.

I started to get really freaked out at the secret group's activities. There were a few things that bothered me.

- **Notifications at three in the morning.** This bothers me because Jasper, my stepson, has a motorbike and he's had one major crash already. Every time the phone pings at that time in the morning, I think it's bad news. I had several mini heart attacks.

- **We were also Maggie's legal carers by this point.** Maggie had an alarm that she would press if anything happened to her that notified someone at the local government's social care team she was in danger. The first thing they do is phone me and ask me to go round to check on her while she is waiting for an ambulance. Again, every time the phone pinged, my next thought, after Jasper, was Maggie.

- **The secret group was where all the girls in the team told the truth.** The whole, depressing, disheartening, truth. The events they hosted, which they boasted about on their public timelines, which were apparently a huge busy, bustling success turned out to be massive failures which nobody attended. And it was only there, in the secret group, that they shared their failures.

- ❖ **My upline, the girl who made money when I made money, was a pushy bitch.** There's no other way to put it. Instead of selling products herself and recruiting and supporting her team members, she was pressuring other people who were below her in the pyramid, to do lots of work. It was the cliché that I didn't think would happen, but clichés are clichés because they are common and real.

It didn't take long for me to get fed up, but I knew that the best way to make money at that time was this pyramid scheme. And to be honest, the sales were going well. I had forty days to make a sales target. I was about to do that. On my thirty-seventh day, I had over five hundred pounds worth of orders to put through the system. But when I logged in, I saw that I had been shut down as an agent.

I did that thing where you think it must be a mistake, so you log out and log back in. I even switched my laptop off and tried again, as if that was going to make any kind of difference! It was correct. I had been cut off. I still had time to make that target, and I was going to do it, but for some reason, they had kicked me out.

I contacted Natalie, the upline. She had gone eerily quiet for a few days and I thought it was simply because she had new recruits and was finally giving me a chance to do the job without constantly bullying me to sell, sell, sell to friends I didn't have. I had half a dozen female mates and some guy from Twitter's girlfriend who I had a coffee with once in my phone book. I'm not a popular person. Although that guy's girlfriend ordered over £100 worth of stuff.

Natalie explained, quite bluntly, that I was out of time. I countered that I wasn't and quoted dates when I had signed up, put in an order etc. She then said she didn't think I would manage to get the orders in time. I told her I had over £500 worth to put through and I had three days left to do it. She then ended the conversation. I was still in the dark and I now had to disappoint my potential buyers.

It was a few days later when I realised what had happened. I had "liked" someone's comment on a Facebook ad for the company where they had criticised the amount of pressure put on people and the lack of support from uplines. Natalie had seen it. She had taken offence and gone against the rules to kick me out. Natalie was watching my every move online to make sure that I was always 100% positive about the brand and that I was liquid sunshine... just like the liars in the secret group. Even a simple Facebook like was taken as a slight and was enough to get me kicked out.

PROFIT MADE: £27

PROFIT I WOULD HAVE MADE IF I HADN'T BEEN KICKED OUT: £157

ICK FACTOR: 5/10

CHANCES OF DOING IT AGAIN: 0/10

A few weeks later, another Facebook ad for that company showed up on my timeline. As I was no longer a part of the scheme or an ambassador for the brand, I left a comment, like the one I had liked, relating my honest opinion of my own experience. Natalie saw it and got verbally abusive, both on the comment and in my private inbox. I had to block and report her.

Sally is still following the pyramid scheme career route. It's going well for her. Sometimes, I buy oven cleaner from her.

6 - THE TIME I MADE FIFTY SHADES OF GREY LOOK FAMILY FRIENDLY

Also known as the point where I realised how vanilla I really am

I consider myself to be open minded. I'm quite accepting of other people's kinks and fetishes, even if I don't have anything too weird going on in my own bedroom. I know a guy with a wife-carrying fetish and another who likes tentacles... I don't judge but it just isn't for me. I do, however, enjoy a mucky book, and have done since I was around fourteen. I remember the first erotica I ever read. It was given to me on holiday by my older sister's friend. I hadn't brought a book with me and she had loads of paperbacks in her suitcase. She handed it to me and told me to read it.

All she said was, 'Here, have a book to read.'

I looked at the cover. The woman with impossibly long red hair was tilting her head back, wearing nothing but a towel, with a look of pure ecstasy on her face. The love interest was wearing tight blue swimming trunks and nothing else. He was one giant muscle-fest and looked a bit like Rob Lowe. I said, 'What kind of book is this?'

Her reply? 'A good book.'

Since then, I've binged on erotica whenever I'm feeling down. Nothing beats the thrill of a thousand calories and an early night with a "good book." Except maybe a thousand calories and actual real-life sex. But I never once saw myself writing a book like that. I read them. I didn't write them. I wrote chick-lit and magical realism and cute cat mysteries. Anthropomorphism was a big feature in my stories. I wrote about talking cats, talking cakes, talking books... there was literally nothing drawing me to erotica, and I had no ambitions to write it. But I kept reading about the successes people had writing smut and as usual, there was nobody to talk me out of it. So, I went for it.

The first thing I did was buy a few books about how to make money writing erotica. There are a lot of them out there. I bought one that said the author had made six figures. Not sure if that was with or without the decimal point... but regardless, he/she was making money so I made that book my bible for a few weeks and referred back to it whenever I needed to reassure myself that this would all be worth it.

The advice in the book was to pick a niche, the kinkier the better. Amazon have certain guidelines, and that's to be expected. For example, no bestiality, no characters under eighteen, no incest, no rape for titillation and no shagging corpses or anything twisted and illegal. There were some grey areas. For example, one writer I know got around the bestiality issue by making some of the animal characters mythical creatures. So, the protagonist could be accepted having sex with a troll or a werewolf, or even a dinosaur. Just not an animal that exists in the real world.

After reading up on unusual fetishes, I realised that some of the kinks people have were kinks I did not know even existed until I started writing erotica. Like dubcon, meaning dubious consent. Or stripper fantasies (I mean women fantasise about being strippers). And then there's a thing called hucow, which basically means human cow. Lactation fetishes. As someone who has breastfed, I can confirm it is the least sexy thing I have ever done. But as Maggie would say, there's a lid for every pot. Somebody somewhere was dying to read more human cow erotica. *gag*

I had a hard time figuring out what I wanted to write. Nothing kinky appealed. On the first day as an erotica writer, I wrote a short story about a girl, Sophia, who has dreams of being a lingerie designer. She dumps her boring boyfriend, gets on a plane to Paris with a suitcase full of her designs and heads to the boutiques of the French capital, hoping that one of the cute little stores will stock her designs. That's when she runs into a mysterious man behind the counter in an empty store. He wants to see the designs modelled (stripper fetish) and when she does that for him, he seduces her (stranger danger fetish) and then they do it in the changing rooms when someone comes into the store (being caught fetish). Afterwards, he disappears and there's only a woman behind the counter. The saleswoman says there's no males working there (humiliation fetish), and the woman accepts her designs and agrees to stock them. At the end, the guy is in his penthouse apartment, thinking about the girl in the boutique, one of many stores he is considering buying and making a part of his worldwide lingerie chain (billionaire fetish), and is getting ready to track her down because he can't get her out of his head.

It seemed very tame compared to some of the books out there that were selling well. I had no idea how to break through that mental barrier, so I forced myself to sit down and write a story about blackmail sex. It was short and nasty. I released the Paris underwear story and the blackmail story on the same day. The Paris underwear story has sold three copies to date. The blackmail story still sells regularly. I honestly think the Paris story had the potential to be re-worked into a good novel, but nastiness sells and as a writer who is a romantic at heart, I'm disappointed. Apparently, women are fantasising about and getting wet over horrible men who blackmail them into violent sex with multiple partners.

I carried on writing various erotica stories that were a more pleasant. Sex with a rock star, sex with a lifeguard who saves the protagonist's life, sex with a firefighter who saves her life, Christmas sex with Santa, ski lodge sex when she's trapped in an avalanche without condoms with a stranger, a sexy reverse harem version of Cinderella with voyeurism and multiple hot princes. Why have one pair of glass slippers when you can have a dozen made of different precious metals and jewels, one from each prince in the kingdom? None of them sold anywhere near as much as the blackmail story. I was devastated. The only way to make money from writing erotica was to write something I was uncomfortable with.

Many people who would love to be writers talk about how embarrassed they would be to show people things they have written. I'd never had that problem until the erotica career began. I was happy to share my work until then. Feeling this uncomfortable was a new experience for me, and it just felt *wrong*. I'm not happy to sit down at the laptop and feel dread about what my fingers are going to create but it is profitable, so there may come a time when I don't have a choice. It's lucrative, easy to do from home and if you have writing skills (I studied creative writing at university and got a distinction), it's the obvious choice for making money.

PROFIT MADE: FIVE FIGURES FROM ALL E-BOOKS – I'M NOT ALLOWED TO SHARE DUE TO AMAZON'S TERMS AND CONDITIONS

ICK FACTOR: 10/10

CHANCES OF DOING IT AGAIN: 10/10

I'm really not comfortable writing dubcon, blackmail erotica. For my next book, I might try tentacles.

7 - THAT TIME I CONVINCED THE WORLD I WAS AN "INFLUENCER"

Also known as how to fake it 'til you make it

I've never been a popular person. I had friends at school, but I was always last picked for teams, on account of being incredibly short and bad at sports and nobody liking me enough to want to spare my feelings. I recall a year, when I was about eight years old, when I went through this phase of not playing with anyone at school. I would stand in the playground, people watching and eating my snack. Nobody invited me to play, and I wasn't pushy enough to force my way into a group of kids. That was the point when I became aware that I wasn't popular, and I started to get lost in my own head and make up stories. I became a compulsive day dreamer, simply because I had no friends to pull me out of it. Knowing what I know now, I think I am probably autistic and that has been a barrier to making meaningful connections.

I never got bullied though. I guess I was too creepy to bully. At secondary school, one of my best friends started a rumour that I was a witch. In response I started a rumour that she was a member of the Church of Satan. Nobody messed with us. They didn't want to be hexed. I had a nice group of misfits that I hung out with at lunch break and on Friday nights and the rest of the time I just kept myself to myself and nobody bothered me. That's why it was such a shock to me when I experienced bullying in the workplace as an adult.

In my first job I was too quiet, wore "weird" clothes, listened to "weird" music, didn't drink, had an older boyfriend...there was always some reason why I wasn't included. Then an older woman, the supervisor as luck would have it, decided I was evil because I'd had an anxiety disorder that prevented me from eating for a while and would therefore corrupt all the other younger girls. She started leaving cut outs from newspapers about the dangers of using laxatives to lose weight on my desk, although I had never been on a diet in my life, never mind had anorexia or bulimia. She would start picking on me for whatever bothered her that day. It was unpleasant and I left.

In my second job I got the silent treatment for two and a half years and they would make ludicrous accusations like I had spat in their tea when it was my turn to make the drinks at break time. The bullying was widespread throughout the office and the boss was the biggest bully of them all.

So, the idea of me being an *influencer* was fucking ridiculous. Nobody likes me. I'm not one of the cool kids.

But Andrea, my physio, who by this time had gotten me back on my feet, was putting ideas in my head about how I could use my Twitter following. As a writer, who had been on Twitter almost since the day Twitter existed, I had amassed quite a following – mostly other writers, but the numbers were high. I had well over 35,000 followers. She said that I really should be doing something to put that "popularity" to good use. It was true. If they all gave me just a pound or a dollar, I'd be quite well off. The wheels started turning in my brain and once again, I was researching how to become an influencer.

When I started to think about it, I realised that the Twitter following was quite impressive. But the problem was that it was 2018 by then and nobody really cared about Twitter, in terms of influencing and PR work. It was all about Instagram. I was 38, almost overweight but not quite yet and my phone is full of pics of my son. Instagram is all about glamour, conventional beauty, filters and living your best life. I certainly wasn't doing that, but I was determined to give it a go.

I started with my author Instagram account. I'd opened it in 2012 and in six years had only accrued 300 followers. Most of them either knew me or were spammers. I started looking at other women's accounts. I learned how to do a flat lay. I started posting pictures of me wearing red lipstick and lots of shine spray on my hair. I wore clothes that hid my bingo wings and double chin. Anything that looked less than perfect got a black and white filter slapped on it. Within a month I had a grid that looked half-decent. I certainly didn't look like the tired mum and stressed out, debt ridden middle-aged woman I felt like and was in reality.

The problem was that I still didn't have many followers, so I started doing what they call **churning**. This means following people, waiting until they follow you back, waiting a couple of weeks to a month and then unfollowing them. The trick is to like a bunch of their pics just as you unfollow. It's also a good idea to like their pics back whenever they like or comment on yours, so they don't notice that you're not following any more. Yes, this is frowned upon. Yes, it's a dickhead move. That's why this book's subtitle is called 10 Totally Legal But Morally Questionable Things I Did To Make Money Online.

I chose carefully. I picked people who weren't bloggers and likely to be watching their follower count. I picked mostly men who were following lots of women – you know the type. They were unlikely to care about a follow back so long as you kept interacting with them. And I didn't follow anyone back when they followed me first, in case they were churning too.

It's something I've criticised others for and I don't recommend it, but it worked. Within a few weeks I had over 5,000 followers and I was getting regular work as an "influencer." I was gifted stationery, umbrellas, heartburn medication and front row tickets to the circus, to name just a few things. Some brands wanted me to share my account demographics with them so they could see who my followers were, their gender, their age and their location. I would reply that this was against my followers' privacy and act as if I was offended. To be fair, they wouldn't have worked with me anyway, had they known the truth.

The important thing is, I didn't pay for any of my followers, and when I feel bad for churning, I take comfort from that fact. I know about half a dozen influencers who did pay for their huge followings and would never admit it publicly. I simply followed and got a follow back. It's entirely up to those people if they want to keep following and all the accounts are genuine people – even if they are men from Morocco who have no interest in the stories, I post to promote the circus and will never buy that umbrella.

For a while, I also took comfort from the fact that I, the girl who was always last picked for teams, and spent many a lunch break standing on her own watching the other kids playing was finally being seen. I was the woman who was bullied in every office job but one and who had always felt like a loser but now I was making money from being popular. I can't tell you how sweet that felt, even if it was fake. Only I knew the truth. The rest of the world just saw my smiling pictures and the paid partnership tags at the top of my posts.

PROFIT MADE: APPROXIMATELY £800 IN CASH, WELL OVER £3000 IN GIFTS

ICK FACTOR: 3/10

CHANCES OF DOING IT AGAIN: UNDECIDED

After a while, I started an account for my dog. He's cute. Why not? He now makes more money than I do as an influencer and promotes pet insurance. The above quoted figures include his income since I am the one who manages his account.

It won't last. I'm 40 now and the older a woman gets, the less visible she becomes. It's a sad reality. There's also the fact that Instagram keep changing their algorithms and they deny that they apply shadow bans to certain accounts, but I believe they do. If they think you've churned or that your account has not grown organically, they can make you disappear from people's timelines. Over the last year, this has happened to me and there's not a damn thing I can do about it.

Now that TikTok is becoming more prominent I might give that a go, but I won't churn. The worst that can happen is that I end up with no followers.

8 – THAT TIME I TRIED LOSING WEIGHT FOR CASH

Also known as the time I realised I had become a psychopath

All good things must come to an end, and the influencer thing came to a head in the most horrible, unpredictable way. This is probably the hardest section of the book to write and for a while, I legally wasn't allowed to write about it.

Ok, I'll be blunt. In 2018, I went for a test at my local hospital. The person who performed the test then broke into my medical records to get my phone number, with a view to contacting me online to initiate inappropriate contact. I had a feeling before this came to light that something was off and my confidentiality had been breached, although it was for another reason, and I had already made a complaint about it. Another woman had pieced together what this guy did, and an investigation followed. That's when they realised that she, I and hundreds of other women had been affected. We got an apology. And that was supposed to be the end of it, but for me, it wasn't.

Having your medical records broken into by someone who was sexually motivated was difficult for me to process. What had he seen? What had he read? Had he been through my psychology file from that time I tried to get help for panic attacks? Did he know every fear, every insecurity, every traumatic event that had ever happened in my life? Was he going to use that to manipulate me into a relationship? Or had he just liked the look of me, taken my phone number and was going to chat me up? The fact I didn't get an explanation or closure or a chance to speak to this guy and ask him what exactly he did and why really cut my emotions to shreds in the months that followed. And the last thing I wanted was to be visible online, where anyone could be anyone.

The worst part is this is something that fucked up my head and I should have had counselling for it. But I couldn't trust anyone in healthcare. And I don't know if I ever will again. It's such an uncomfortable subject that any time I have tried to reach out to a friend to talk about it, they didn't want to know. Healthcare workers are this elite group of people who have unquestioned respect and are treated like Gods. But they are human, and humans make mistakes. Sometimes they hurt others.

I didn't sell my knickers. I didn't join a pyramid scheme or start gambling. I didn't write blogs about Azerbaijan. And I certainly didn't want to have the high-profile online presence that influencers have any more. I didn't know what to do, so I ate a lot of unhealthy foods, got very angry over things that didn't matter and called the Samaritans quite a few times saying I wanted to jump in front of a train. I didn't really want that. I just wanted to feel normal again. The only person I could talk to be the tutor from my distance learning course, so I did, and she let me lean on her a few times. We talked about processing feelings and how to describe emotions with creative writing and how to edit them so that they're coherent and readable, not just some rambling mess. I ended up getting a distinction for the year and then I quit.

During that time, I also went back to a normal 9 to 5 job. This time I worked in a bank. It was the start of me getting my old self back. I was going to be respectable again. No more professional gambling or catering to fetishes. The old Amie-Jade was still in there somewhere and since my back problem was about 80% gone, I was going to make money the old-fashioned way. I was so excited.

But this is me we're talking about and of course it wasn't going to last.

A few months before I got the job, I had applied for a place on a prime-time gameshow on TV. I got an audition and I cleared it with my boss. He let me change a shift so I could go. On the day that the audition arrived, my grandfather died. I still went, rocked it and got a place on the show. Then I went to work and put in the rest of my shift. My boss was confused. He didn't understand how anyone could work on the day a family member had died, let alone go for a big audition and succeed. I hadn't even cried. What was wrong with me?

The answer is nothing. I'm just very good at compartmentalising. It's a skill I picked up at some point in the last few years when I was doing all sorts of despicable things in the name of making a few quid. You might even notice that as this book has progressed, I became less affected and apologetic. By the time 2019 had arrived, and I'd gone through a period of suicidal ideation and had dealt with a string of failures and disappointments, mostly alone or with only Fraser for support, I had hardened. I'd do my crying when I was ready, in the privacy of my own home, on my terms. Nobody was going to tell me when I should or should not grieve for my grandfather.

Perhaps that's a little bit psychopathic. If I was writing a psychopathic character in fiction, I would probably write someone who could grieve at a time of their choosing, like I did. None of the other characters would understand them, but the backstory would show that it's a survival mechanism.

To cut a long story short, my boss gave me a really hard time that day. I think he was trying to draw the tears out of me. He pulled me into his office, denied me every holiday request I had made, told me he was going to choose my holidays, said he was going to restrict my time off to no more than one or two days at a time even though all the other employees could take up to a fortnight in one break, and told me to get used to hardly ever seeing my son and missing all his birthdays and school concerts etc.

I told him to fuck off.

Not really. I wish I had. I'm maybe a little bit psychopathic now but I'm not verbally aggressive and I don't like being nasty to people, even when provoked. I simply removed myself from the room, picked up my handbag and walked out. I returned an hour later with an unwashed uniform in a carrier bag and handed it back to him without a word while he pouted and looked like he was ready to cry. Then I had chocolate for breakfast every morning until after the funeral.

I think I might be unemployable now because I'm sure most people would have stayed and just complained to their friends about having a shit boss. I wasn't prepared to sell my time to someone who was going to treat me like his bitch when I am at my lowest ebb.

Within two months, I was overweight. It's the first time in my life that I've been overweight without having a baby in my womb. I had gone back to writing smut and occasionally doing mystery shopping jobs and was broke. When I was looking at diets online, I found out about a diet gambling site.

The temptation was too much. I signed up.

The basic idea behind these gambling sites is that you bet on your own health. You sign up, weigh in and you place your bet. They have a pot that gets split between all the winners. So essentially, if there are 30 people playing and they all bet $10, the pot is $300. All those who hit their weight loss target share the $300 between them and those who didn't reach their goal weight get nothing. The site takes a cut to cover costs and pay for competition prizes, which is usually 10% but sometimes as much as 25%. So long as you hit your target, you will receive at least your stake back.

Although I was overweight, I still didn't have that much weight to lose. I signed up to a bet that lasted six months and gambled that I would lose 10% of my body weight. I also signed up to a good old-fashioned calorie counting site. This would be easy money.

For the first month, the weight came off steadily. I had hit my monthly goal by the 17th of the month. Then the wheels came off because I was still thoroughly depressed. I still hadn't processed what happened with the confidentiality breach, I was still grieving (although at this point, I wasn't sure who or what I was grieving for) and I was eating for comfort, because food was the only thing that made me feel good. It was the only pleasure I had.

I often think that perhaps if I was a drinker, I would have been an alcoholic by this point, or at least have had a major problem. It's a good thing I never touch it.

If I had a bad day, I would eat. If I had a good day, I would celebrate by eating. If I was bored, I would eat. If I was lonely, I would eat. If my books had sold, I would celebrate by eating. If my books hadn't sold, I would commiserate by eating. It was all I wanted to do and nothing else gave me the comfort that sugar and fat did. I had to really struggle to break those habits and I missed my next two monthly goals.

My other issue with this was that all the other participants were in a group chat on the site's app. I could see what other people were doing, when they won, when they lost, what they were posting, how they felt about it. That first month, when I won, I couldn't take any joy in my victory because thousands of other people lost. They didn't just lose their bets. They lost hope. Many of them quit, others struggled on, but they had to come to terms with the fact that not only had they not lost weight and were still unhappy with the bodies they were living in, but they were also being confronted with the joy from others who had succeeded. It felt cruel.

This felt nothing like the gambling I had done at the very beginning of my problems when I was matched betting. That was a sure thing. Matched betting wasn't really gambling because you couldn't lose. I was always going to extract a profit from the gambling websites. This really was a gamble. It wasn't being regulated by anyone either. Some players were betting hundreds of dollars on multiple games on the site, and then losing because they were doing what nature tells them to do – eat.

The good that came out of it was that I lost seven pounds during the first three months, which made me officially a healthy weight again, even if I hadn't reached my goal. I would probably have continued and tried to finish the six-month bet, but Covid 19 had made an appearance in the world by then and in month four, I gave up because I couldn't get to a supermarket to buy fresh food. Fraser and Bruce had underlying health issues meaning they had to shield, and I shielded with them. I won a total of $18.15 from my bet, but I had gambled $140.

Despite my reservations about the morality of this game, I started another bet after writing this chapter. I decided to try again because I know how much money other people who stuck with the game and won their bets got for the last six-month game – the one I quit. They made a profit of over $100, and they reached their goal weight. That's what I wanted for myself. This time, I won and made £300 in profit – I clearly picked the right game to play.

PROFIT MADE: £316 (read on...)

ICK FACTOR: 5/10

CHANCES OF DOING IT AGAIN: 9/10

I do still feel sad for those who don't make their goals, but let's be honest. I can't throw away the chance to be happy and healthy because there are other people in the world who aren't. And once again, I sound like a psychopath.

9 – THAT TIME I SOLD BOOKS FULL OF BLANK PAGES

Also known as the time I got my shit together while the rest of the world lost theirs

We're right up to date now and onto the latest money-making scheme that I tried. A lot has changed since the autumn of 2015 when I was broke, lonely and scared. Now we're in lockdown and I'm broke, lonely and scared for a whole load of different reasons. At the time of writing, I am lucky enough to have avoided Covid 19 and I'm thankful for that.

Lock down was a re-boot for me. While many were desperate to return to a normal life, I realised that I didn't want to do that. Normal sucked. My life was nothing like I thought it would be. That, coupled with the fact that I was turning 40 in 2020, made me question what I really wanted out of life. Was it more of the same? Shitty jobs, shitty bosses and totally legal but morally questionable side-hustles? That's not what I want and it's not what I'm going to do any more.

In my dream life, I'm happy, healthy, writing books that excite me and making a passive income with a business I'm happy to talk to people about, without hiding details and pretending I'm just a housewife. And I'm going to get all that.

I started a workout regime, to strengthen my back, and everything else if I'm honest. I've gotten really unfit over the last few years because I've been out of action.

I got a short story accepted and published in a Scots language anthology – my first acceptance in over a decade and my first fiction acceptance. It was the story I wrote during the time I was trying to process the confidentiality breach. My tutor helped me to process injustice and write about it in a coherent way.

I signed up for some courses with Harvard's online program. Then I signed up for courses with the University of Barcelona. And with the California Institute of the Arts. At least if I ever get another job, I won't look like I wasted my time.

I wrote several summer holiday romances – sweet but thought-provoking stories about women having holiday flings with memorable men. There is no blackmail involved. Or tentacles for that matter.

I started a business I am proud of, even if it is morally questionable and raises a few eyebrows when I tell people about it and that's what this chapter is about.

So, during lockdown, Scotland had a glorious spring heatwave. I spent a morning sunbathing and chatting online to Toni, an American woman who ran a course I took a couple of years ago. She is also an online hustler, always jumping from one money making scheme to the next. She's done it all, from pyramid schemes, to blogging, to designing t-shirts. She is someone who would never judge me. Toni told me that currently she is working on publishing low content books online and she is loving it. I said something like, "Oh, that's great!" I had no idea what Toni was talking about.

A couple of weeks later, I was thinking about that conversation and I did an online search for low content books. She had been talking about notebooks, diaries, journals, colouring books. Anything you could self-publish that didn't involve writing fell into that category. Sometimes it was simply a paperback book full of lined pages. And people were cleaning up doing this, people like Toni and people like me.

There isn't really an interesting story here, or a downside – yet. Perhaps in a couple of years I'll update this book and tell you that I've transformed myself into a millionaire by doing this, or perhaps there will be a dark side to low content publishing. But so far, I've published 250 books, ranging from blank lined pages, to dream diaries with half a dozen prompts on each page (and a bunch of lines), gratitude journals and a perfume maker's logbook – something I could have used when I was a perfumer. I'm particularly proud of my witch's spell notebook, a nod to my teenage self, the girl who was happy to let her friend spread a rumour she was a witch, so she didn't get bullied. There are plenty of spooky men and women out there who love that kind of thing.

And then there's puzzle books. That's where most of my money comes from now. Sudoku, wordsearches, crosswords, mazes. I invested in some puzzle generating software and for the word games, I do a lot of online research. It's great preparation for my appearance on the prime time TV quiz show, which is happening soon.

In the first edition of this book, I shared that a quarter of my publishing income was coming from those blank books. I was one month into my low content journey then. I'm nine months down the line now and 95% comes from puzzle books and diaries. I believe I could really make something of this business. I only have around 250 online now. If I have 1500 or 2000, it's a full-time, passive income, that will allow me to write my sweet adventure romances without the pressure of trying to make a living from writing.

To date, I've only had a couple of negative reviews; one when the woman complained that the book she purchased was "basic", but the description clearly states that it contains blank, lined pages. Facts are facts and if she had read the description before her purchase, she would have not been disappointed. The other was a guy who posted a picture of the interior of the blank diary and said, "uh, it's like this." Sorry mate, it won't have your plans and such filled in already. It's a blank diary!

PROFIT MADE: THREE FIGURES IN THE FIRST MONTH, AVERAGING £450 A MONTH RIGHT NOW

ICK FACTOR: 1/10

CHANCES OF DOING IT AGAIN: 10/10

10 – THAT TIME I WROTE A BOOK ABOUT ALL MY ICKY EXPERIENCES
Also known as catharsis

And now we're up to date. This book was first published in August 2020 when we were tentatively emerging from lockdown number one in Scotland, although I had a suspicion that Covid 19 is nowhere near gone yet. I'm editing it in March 2021 and updating with the latest figures and surprise, surprise. We've been back in lockdown since last December.

In August 2020 I was working my way through these courses I signed up for, getting ready to publish those sweet romances I wrote last spring and I was cautiously optimistic about the future of my notebook business. Everything was going well.

Then Maggie passed away. We haven't been told it was Covid 19, although I think it was. She caught whatever infection killed her in hospital. I hadn't spoken to her in a while. We had a falling out because a gay couple moved in next door to her, and she was homophobic in the truest sense of the word. She was terrified of them. I found it extremely hard to be reasonable about her fears.

Social worker: She's scared of them

Amie-Jade: I know, but that's no excuse for how she's behaving

Social worker: She's from another time

Amie-Jade: No, she's not. She is alive right now. This is her time. She's not a bloody time traveller

I wish I had treated her with compassion because fear must be met with kindness. Anger won't make anyone less frightened. Sadly, I took an angry approach, and I will always regret it because we didn't get a chance to make it up before she died. Instead, Fraser and I weren't even told that she had died until almost a week afterwards, by neighbours, and we weren't told about the funeral. I feel like it's no more than I deserved. I should have been there for her, like she was for me.

I think Maggie would have approved of my notebook business, especially since I am putting those creative juices to good use to design all the covers myself. I just wish I had gotten the chance to tell her about it.

The local taxi driver had gone to the funeral and dealt with registering her death. She had built up quite a rapport with him and his family and they had been good friends to her. I was keen to know her real age. He said she was listed on the death certificate as 93. I wondered why she was so fixated on that age, but I guess I'll never know. Maybe she knew that was the last age she would ever be and was just waiting for it.

So, which of these schemes do I have plans to try again? I'm definitely going to keep publishing notebooks and journals. I have a lot of plans for new erotic fiction, and I will dive into matched betting again every Christmas. As for the rest? No.

I turned 40 in July 2020 and did a lot of thinking about my life. I just kept thinking about all the things I've done in the last few years and I felt unbelievably sad.

So, I've sat down to write about them. I can't believe I'm writing a memoir and I'm only 40. I'm not a famous person, or a successful one. I'm not an interesting person, but I feel that if there's any way I can pass this knowledge on and make people laugh or give someone else a realistic view of a money-making scheme, it's been worthwhile.

And who knows? Maybe I'll make a few quid.

Copyright © S Milligan August 2020

First published as an eBook in August 2020 as 10 Totally Legal But Morally Questionable Ways I Made Money Online or The Diary of A Train Wreck

Second edition published as an e-book and paperback March 2021

All rights reserved. No part of this book may be reproduced or used in any manner without prior written consent from the copyright owner except for in a quotation or book review.

For permissions email info@laceydearie.com

www.ingramcontent.com/pod-product-compliance
Lightning Source LLC
Chambersburg PA
CBHW050253220526
45465CB00002B/661